FU MANCHU AND THE 'YELLOW PERIL':
THE MAKING OF A RACIST MYTH

Jenny Clegg

𝑡𝑏

Trentham Books

First published in 1994 by Trentham Books Limited

Trentham Books Limited
Westview House
734 London Road
Oakhill
Stoke-on-Trent
Staffordshire
England ST4 5NP

Picture Acknowledgements

1.2 and 1.3. Copyright © by Universal Pictures, a division of Universal City Studios, Inc. Courtesy of MCA Publishing Rights, a division of MCA, Inc.

1.4. Reproduced by kind permission of John Warner Publications.

2.2. Picture Collection, The Branch Libraries, The New York Public Library.

2.6. Hulton Deutsch Collection.

3.2. The Trustees of the Imperial War Museum, London. (Q2695).

3.4. Reproduced by kind permission of Stoll Moss Theatres.

4.2. Reproduced by kind permission of Paolo Hu.

4.4. Reproduced by kind permission of George Ping.

4.6. Reproduced by kind permission of W. Tay.

Every effort has been made to reach copyright holders. The publishers would be glad to hear from anyone whose rights they have unknowingly infringed.

Designed by Trentham Print Design Limited, Chester and printed by Bemrose Shafron Limited, Chester.

FU MANCHU AND THE 'YELLOW PERIL':
THE MAKING OF A RACIST MYTH

Contents

Acknowledgements

I would like to thank all my friends in Manchester's Chinatown from whom I have learned so much.

I would also like to thank Richard Harris, Keith Webb, Maria Noble and the Institute of Race Relations for their comments and advice on earlier drafts of this work which helped to bring this book to publication.

Preface

This book aims to investigate the systematic nature of racist ideology through a critical analysis of the myth of the 'yellow peril', epitomised by the character of Dr. Fu Manchu, the stereotypical mysterious, threatening and unknowable Oriental master-villain. This character was first created by the writer, Sax Rohmer, in a series of short stories published in 1912, and the character was further demonised through numerous B-films, dating from the 1920s to the 1960s.

Fu Manchu became familiar as the personification of the 'yellow peril'. What follows will show how this particular racist myth arose.

From the 1880s, and growing to screaming pitch in the 1920s, the press poured out a ceaseless stream of innuendoes and slanders about life in the tiny Chinatowns of London and Liverpool, and the proliferation of the 'opium dens'. The small Chinese community suffered increasing harassment both from the local population and the authorities, as the idea of the 'yellow peril' played upon fears that the world was about to be swamped by floods of Chinese who would destroy Western culture with their strange Oriental ways. The 'threat' of cheap labour from China was magnified with tales of drug trafficking, secret societies and seductions of young white women.

The image of Fu Manchu using a secret potion to lure young girls into his power, makes the very threatening link between sex and drugs. Yet it was the British who, in the nineteenth century, forced opium on the Chinese.

The opium trade, reinforced by two wars, was to drain the Chinese economy, hastening the collapse of the Imperial order. On the one hand the Chinese peasants, traditionally tied to the land and to their village communities, were forced to migrate or starve; and on the other hand, China was opened to the British to recruit 'coolie' labour for work in its colonies. This mobile force of cheap labour, with no choice but to work for subsistence wages, paid by European employers at rates often below one fifth of a European wage, became a 'yellow peril' exploited by employers to break strikes in Britain as elsewhere in the Western world.

Why did the Chinese, themselves the victims of the opium trade, become labelled as the perpetrators of drug trafficking? Why, in the early part of the twentieth century did the numerically insignificant, peaceable Chinese community in Britain, which had a no more than average crime rate, become the focus of public attention and the subject of continual investigation by the police, the press and the politicians? These are some of the questions explored in this book.

The systematic fabrication of this particular mythology of race within Britain not only obscured the roots of China's poverty and its inability at this time to feed and clothe its population, but also fostered loyalty to the British Empire. Fears of the Asian threat built upon certain assumptions regarding inherent racial characteristics. The depiction of Asian vice provided a backdrop for British virtue. The Fu Manchu films abound with blatant colonial imagery. The notion of danger from the Orient is used to heighten identification with the white upper-class hero and to convince the audience of the necessity of Empire as the sole guarantee of security. Both press and film were unleashing a continual stream of derogatory images upon the British public, whilst in China the seeds of opposition were planted and a revolutionary movement began to grow.

But there is yet another side to the story. Whilst British troops were used again and again to suppress progressive elements in China, protecting Britain's privileges to exploit the resources, including the labour of the country, there existed within Britain a recurrent movement of opposition to the policies of colonialism and imperialism.

The conflicts and divisions between the British and Chinese seamen in 1911, compared with the international solidarity which developed in 1926/7 and which began to prove threatening to the British state, offer invaluable insights into the nature of racism.

The themes and images which shaped the myth of the 'yellow peril' in the past persist in popular culture today. The Chinese in Britain are often portrayed in the press and on TV as a closed conspiratorial group, masterminded behind the scenes by international Triad drug barons. The reality is more that of a scattered and isolated community, vulnerable to racist attacks, both physical and verbal, as the 'yellow peril' myth is kept alive by racist organisations and politicians and by the media.

For the most part ignored and neglected by the authorities, the Chinese in Britain, when brought to the attention of the public, are often identified as an 'immigration problem'. This is increasingly the case as the take-over of Hong Kong by China from the British colonial administration in 1997 draws closer. The underlying issues here and the real concerns of the Chinese in Britain today can be neither appreciated nor responded to, however, until the roots of the 'yellow peril' myth are fully exposed.

Introduction:
using this book as a teaching aid

This book sets out to unravel the myth of the 'yellow peril' and to explore its political, social, economic and ideological roots and dimensions against a background of the real lives of the Chinese communities in Britain and of the historical relations between Britain and China. The book is designed to raise awareness of racism through promoting an understanding of the present as an outcome of the past. History serves to highlight the present-day situation, experiences and perspectives of the Chinese community in our midst, and contributes to a deeper understanding of the social dynamics which shape relations in present-day multi-racial Britain.

The book fosters a process of 'unlearning' racism by challenging racist stereotypes and providing a basis and perspective from which to begin to tackle complex issues of race and class.

Chapter One presents the familiar racial myth for examination, identifying its main themes and assumptions, and contrasting the images with the lives of the Chinese in Britain. It also draws attention to the malign press the Chinese received, so as to sow seeds of doubt in the mind of the student as to the acceptability of the image of the 'yellow peril' and to encourage a questioning approach.

Chapter Two looks at the idea of the 'yellow peril' and how it came about, tracing its roots to the opium and 'coolie' trade. By placing the myth in its historical and international context to expose its political and economic roots, this chapter aims to enable the reader to see not only *how* but also *why* racist ideas arose as a legitimation of colonialism through the assertion of superiority of the British.

Adopting a historical approach which portrays the colonised as victims who passively submitted to the horrors of colonial exploitation, has the danger of reinforcing racial stereotypes with further stereotypical views of their countries of origin as backward, uncivilised, poverty-stricken and so on. What has to be challenged are the basic assumptions of inferiority and superiority and this book does so through its historically verified account of how the Chinese resisted conditions of exploitation.

Chapter Three seeks to show how the racist myth operated in concrete situations, that is, in relation to the dynamics between different interest groups or classes at a particular juncture and also to appreciate under what conditions a positive perception of the Chinese on the part of the British people might become possible.

Closer analysis of the conditions shows how the 'yellow peril' notion flourished. The social and political processes in British society underlying its persistence together with a consideration, within the international context, of the different responses on the part of British labour towards cheap Chinese labour — of conflict and competition for the most part, but also of solidarity at certain critical moments — gives the student new evidence. By showing above all that there was another side to the story, not only the development of the national resistance movement in China but also the recurrent, if weak, element within British politics which did not go along with colonial and imperialist policies, this chapter provides a particular class perspective and new insights which may facilitate the 'unlearning' of racism.

The ultimate test of the book lies in the transferability of the learning — the application of what can be drawn from this story of conflict and solidarity between British and Chinese people to the present-day problems and conditions of multi-racial Britain.

The examination in Chapter Four of the elements that went into the creation of the 'yellow peril' myth, reveals how the same underlying themes, images and assumptions about the Chinese persist in present-day popular culture, in clear contradiction to the reality of the lives of the scattered and isolated community. The hidden consequences of the perpetuation of such myths are investigated and exposed.

It is generally thought that the Chinese do not suffer from racial harassment to the same extent as other ethnic minority groups in Britain. The fact is that whilst the Chinese survive for the most part in an environment which scarcely acknowledges their existence, this climate of ignorance serves as a thin veneer for hostility, as fear of the 'yellow peril' is kept alive by the media and by right-wing politicians. As restaurant and chip-shop owners, the Chinese are particularly vulnerable to racist abuse and attacks as the evidence shows.

The learning process is concerned to promote reasoning as a basis for adoption of attitudes and values. It is hoped that this learning can be extended to clarify present-day problems of racism and critically to appraise contemporary racism and the interests it serves.

A final worksheet is provided to further consolidate learning, evaluation and self-assessment. It offers questions and quotations to guide structured discussion or exercises so that the following can be assessed:

a) changes in attitudes and perceptions (self-assessment);

b)   the ability to apply what has been learned to issues of relevance in today's Britain e.g. criminalisation and drugs, immigration control and unemployment (discussion);

c)   the ability to tackle complex definitions in the relationship between race and class; to understand the various ways in which racism operates by legitimising colonialism and discrimination; by promoting the 'divide and rule' of the working classes, so weakening their struggle against the employers, and by encouraging scapegoating as a safe outlet for the social tensions within the capitalist system (small group work; individual written work).

Anti-racist education is not just a matter of supplementing the existing curriculum — adding some references to the ethnic minorities in Britain; adding the history of Africa and Asia to British history. Adopting an anti-racist perspective means learning new things about ourselves. This involves overhauling the entire curriculum, and this in turn requires the development of new learning resources. Unfortunately, few of the existing educational materials on racism even touch upon the experience of the Chinese. Yet the Chinese are the third largest visible ethnic minority in this country and they make up one fifth of the world's population.

This book aims at filling this gap. It provides material for looking at many issues central to the sociology of Race, linking in with other sociological questions such as: stereotyping; the role of the media in creating 'folk devils' and 'moral panics'. It uses a variety of evidence: statements by politicians, statistics, newspaper reports, case studies, trade union resolutions, and other contemporary sources.

The book is appropriate across a range of courses which aim to develop skills of critical analysis and evaluation and to promote a better understanding of the causes and effects of racism. It is designed to be flexible in its application: it may be used as a complete short course in itself or for providing a unit on racism in a wider context; it may be adapted to provide the basis for a one day workshop; or it may be used for self-study. Each chapter is accompanied by a worksheet of activities for individual study or for discussion and written work in a small group.

Learning objectives

This book seeks to enable learners:

- ☐ to identify and criticise the assumptions that underlie stereotypical views of Chinese people;

- ☐ to gain some insight into and understanding of the background of ethnic minority communities in Britain, through a consideration of the history and the present-day experience of the Chinese;

- ☐ to recognise the significance of some of the major events in the history of relations between Britain and China and to understand some of the main reasons for the development of the national revolutionary movement in China;

- ☐ to develop awareness of the impact of British imperialism on China and the effects and consequences of political domination and economic underdevelopment, particularly as a cause of migration;

- ☐ to understand how racism operates in legitimising colonialism, promoting division among the working classes and encouraging scapegoating as a release of social tensions;

- ☐ to understand the role of the media, its content and influence, in fostering racial stereotyping, shaping attitudes and values and defining issues of public concern;

- ☐ to develop a new perspective on the issue of racism and a deeper appreciation of the relationship between race and class, through an evaluation of the conditions of conflict and solidarity between British and Chinese workers.

Chapter 1

FU MANCHU:
THE 'YELLOW PERIL' INCARNATE

What does the myth of the 'yellow peril' consist of? In what way was it a myth? How did it compare with the lives of Chinese in Britain?

Fu Manchu — the films and the stories

1.1. Film poster from the
Drums of Fu Manchu

The image of Fu Manchu, personification of the 'yellow peril', has been absorbed deeply into English popular consciousness. He is the stereotypical Oriental villain — a sinister mastermind bent on world domination.

The character of the 'evil yellow doctor' was created by Sax Rohmer in a thriller series published in 1912, which warned of Asian hordes on the verge of sweeping through Europe, threatening the overthrow of Western civilisation. As with every villain, there is an opposing hero, and while Fu Manchu represented the yellow rabble about to swamp Europe, Sir Denis Nayland-Smith was the figure of 'Western acumen pitted against Eastern cunning'.

1

Rohmer built his stories around the themes of sex, drugs and crime, using images of conspiratorial Chinese, ruined virgins and tenacious British policemen. The formula proved immensely popular in America as well as Britain, and a second series of short stories was followed by a spate of films, a radio series, a comic strip and later a TV series.

Rohmer introduces Fu Manchu unequivocally as the representative of the Asian threat to the West:

> Imagine a person, tall, lean and feline, high-shouldered, with a brow like Shakespeare and a face like Satan, a close-shaven skull and long magnetic eyes a of true cat-green. Invest him with all the cruel cunning of an entire Eastern race accumulated in one giant intellect, with all the resources, if you will, of a wealthy government, which however, has already denied all knowledge of his existence. Imagine that awful being, and you have a mental picture of Dr Fu Manchu, the yellow peril incarnate in one man.

The Insidious Dr. Fu Manchu.[1]

"Your mind is completely under my control."

2

THE FILMS

1921	The Yellow Claw
1923	The Mystery of Dr. Fu Manchu
1924	The Further Mysteries of Dr. Fu Manchu
1929	The Mysterious Dr. Fu Manchu
1930	The Return of Dr. Fu Manchu
1931	Daughter of the Dragon
1932	The Mask of Fu Manchu*
1940	Drums of Fu Manchu
1955	The Adventures of Fu Manchu
1965	The Face of Fu Manchu**
1966	The Brides of Fu Manchu**
1967	The Vengeance of Fu Manchu**
1968	The Blood of Fu Manchu**
*	with Boris Karloff
**	with Christopher Lee

Rohmer never visited the Far East — he was a small-time freelance journalist, barely scraping a living from writing music hall sketches and songs, with a certain reputation for interest in the occult. The inspiration for his stories came from superficial contact with East London's small Chinese community. In 1911, the police were carrying out an investigation of crime in the Limehouse area, where the Chinese owner of a gambling house had come under suspicion for connections with a drugs syndicate. Rohmer was commissioned by a magazine to cover the story.

Nothing came of the investigation, but Rohmer, having spent some weeks hanging around the streets and cafes of Chinatown, managed to pick up certain notions about the Chinese and their social organisations — the large kinship-based 'mutual aid' networks on which they relied for support and survival. For Rohmer, those 'sworn brotherhoods' were filled with mystery and intrigue. On the basis of a little knowledge he began to speculate:

> Supposing, I asked myself, a number of those sinister organisations — were in turn responsible to the direction of some a super-society. Such

Opposite: 1.2. *Daughter of the Dragon*
'Your mind is completely under my control...'
Eastern cunning is pitted against Western acumen

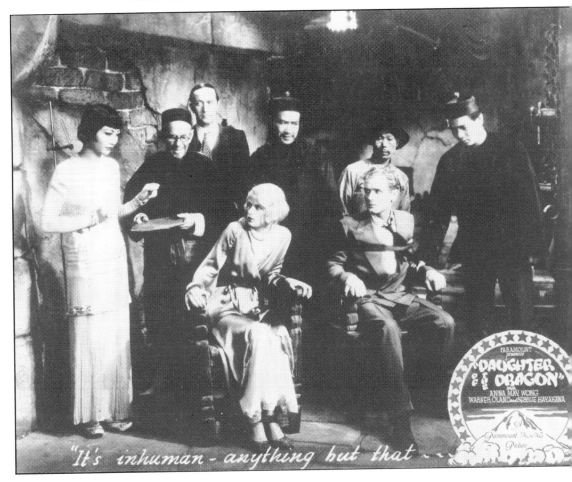

"It's inhuman - anything but that..."

1.3. *Daughter of the Dragon*
'The swamping of the white world by the yellow hordes might well be the price of our failure'

a society would hold the power to upset governments, perhaps change the very course of civilisation... I began to wonder what the president of my imaginary super-society would be like, what manner of man could dominate that world-wide shadowy empire...[2]

Fu Manchu is the powerful leader of a rebellious yellow mob — the scum of Chinatown's opium dens, rough waterfronts, secret societies and heathen religious brotherhoods. In him the qualities of being exotic and evil are bound together, connecting the characteristics of the Chinese with crime, vice and cruelty. He characterises the threat of the yellow hordes and links this with the lecherous impulses of 'Chinamen' towards white women. He also personifies the dangers of combining Western science with the ancient customs of the Chinese, for Fu Manchu is Western-educated. His villainy is a product of Chinese tradition and so, not bound by the 'norms' of the rational civilised West, his behaviour is beyond reason: he belongs to a 'race of ancestor-worshippers which is capable of anything'. This evil genius uses Western science to enhance his powers of super-hypnosis and develops a secret potion which induces cataleptic trance, giving him control over his opponents.

Fu Manchu is an indication of the rising tide of Asian politics:

> He is no ordinary criminal. He is the greatest genius which the powers of evil have put on earth for centuries...and his mission is to pave the way!...He is the advance agent of a movement so epoch-making that not one Britisher, and not one American in fifty thousand has ever dreamed of.[3]

In *The Mystery of Dr. Fu Manchu*, Sir Denis Nayland-Smith of Scotland Yard is in pursuit of the 'devil doctor'. The urgency is extreme, and Smith acts:

> not in the interests of the British government merely, but in the interests of the entire white race, and I honestly believe — though I pray I may be wrong — that its survival depends largely upon the success of my mission.[4]

Rohmer made a fortune — close to two million dollars from the books alone. Small wonder that in signing his name, he customarily wrote the 'S' for Sax with a dollar sign!

The Limehouse Legend

Before World War One, a small Chinatown existed in the East London neighbourhood of Pennyfields and Limehouse Causeway. Rohmer's books played no small part in creating its legendary reputation:

> At the mere mention of the name 'Limehouse' what images inevitably spring to mind? A vista of dark streets, shadowy yellow-faced forms, a brief flash of a knife-blade, a scream in the night, a bloated corpse fished up from the murky waters of the Thames...the neighbourhood formed a no-man's land which honest citizens hesitated to penetrate after dark. Police honoured the area with double patrols: the precise toll of lives in that sombre labyrinth cannot be estimated. The region housed an Asian community, firmly entrenched and largely criminal, which lived by laws foreign to, and older than, the laws of England.

Chinatown as portrayed by Sax Rohmer, in the words of his biographer, Cay Van Ash.[5]

The First Chinese in Britain

Apart from a handful of diplomats and students, Chinese people first came to Britain as seamen. One of the earliest accounts of Chinese people in Britain was in 1851, when it was reported that there were 78 Chinese-born residents living in London.

The opening of the China trade to British and other European merchants increased the need for Chinese seamen, who were initially recruited by the British East India Company. In 1868, the Liverpool shippers, Alfred and Philip Holt, started the first direct steamship company from Europe to China, and Chinese seamen were more frequently to be seen in British ports such as Liverpool, Cardiff and London.

In London, a Chinatown began to develop from the 1880s, in the Limehouse district bordering the West India Docks. The community was still very small, but enough to populate the two streets of

1.5. One of the first Chinese to study in Britain

Pennyfields and Limehouse Causeway. Many were non-residents — so-journers intent on returning home once it was financially worthwhile to do so. Others had jumped ship to find jobs, but kept in close touch with their origins, opening boarding houses, grocery shops and eating houses catering for the flow of Chinese sailors and the handful of students. These places provided a sense of community for the largely transient population, and a safe haven where they could meet and relax.

> Taken altogether, the Chinaman in Limehouse is a most peaceable, inoffensive and harmless character. He is picturesque in a region where it is sorely needed.
>
> An English visitor, 1900.[6]

The 1901 census records show a population of 387 Chinese-born residents, but Chinese street names such as Ming Street and Canton Street suggest that the Chinese made a visible impact in the Limehouse area.

With the opening of laundries and restaurants catering for the British, the community grew to 1,319 in 1911. By 1921, it had reached 2,419.

1.4. 'On board a Junk' c. 1868 (J. Thompson)

1.6 Chinatown, London 1911

Isolated from their surrounding neighbourhood by language, culture and the transience of their stay, the Chinese formed a small, sealed community. But although they were numerically insignificant, they were easily identifiable and their alien characteristics were occasionally emphasised by their strange forms of recreation, including gambling and opium-taking, and their general tendency to stay within their own ethnic group. In the eyes of some, they constituted a social threat, not least because the population was overwhelmingly male, which meant that Chinese men often took up with white women. All this received publicity in the popular press, arousing the curiosity and often the hostility of the British.

In 1906 in Liverpool, Holt's Blue Funnel line was employing nearly 2,000 Chinese seamen, of whom 120 on average were always in the docks. The rest of the community was made up of 224 residents, of whom 15 were married to, or living with white women. Yet in that year, the local press contains evidence of a major scare over the 'yellow peril', their 'perverted women' and 'sinister offspring'.

There were allegations of crime and violence and the seduction of underage girls through drink and opium; tales of hypnotic powers; and claims that nearly all the Chinese shops and businesses were blinds for gambling and opium-smoking, with the conditions of the boarding-houses reported as indescribably filthy and overcrowded.

In an article on Chinese vice in England, Claude Blake of the *Sunday Chronicle* insisted that the 'notoriously prolific' Chinese were turning Liverpool into a 'yellow town'. Claiming that they were 'not fitted to be a part of civilised white society', Blake raised the alarm:

> Is this open sore to be allowed to fester in a white community? Remember this, the Chinese are in close touch with one another all over the world, and when they hear from their countrymen that England is a good place where they are allowed to do as they like, they will come here in droves...[7]

Liverpool's City Council responded to the allegations with a Commission of Inquiry into the morals, habits and economic aspects of the Chinese presence. The city's Chief Constable, however, saw no cause for concern regarding the observation of sanitary regulations; gambling existed but for small stakes, and there had been only one incident of a violent quarrel over a debt; and whilst opium-smoking was 'no doubt common amongst them, 'it amounts to no offence against the law, and no crimes due to it have come to the knowledge of the police'.[8]

The Commission of Inquiry had to report that the Chinese were the embodiment of public order: Chinatown's Pitt Street was 'long noted as a street down which a woman might walk without molestation' and the Chinese 'led orderly and peaceable lives and always maintained cordial relations with their English neighbours.'

1.7. Ah Tack's Licensed Boarding House

But the 'yellow peril' scare had done its damage: relations between the English and the Chinese had been poisoned. Whenever a new Chinese business opened, there were hostile demonstrations by local residents; the Chinese suffered constant physical harassment and continued libel as the press plugged away, with more stories of imputed immorality.

In March 1906, five Chinamen were charged with illicit gambling. Significantly, the magistrate's annoyance at their presence in the dock was directed not at them but at the police. This was clear from his observation that:

> ...there were no complaints from the incidents as to annoyance caused by the tenant of the shop and his visitors. These foreigners were only doing what they were permitted to do in their own country...It is a pity under the circumstances that the authorities could not shut their eyes to it. In all probability playing did go on at this house for money in small sums but...it was not a very serious thing...[9]

From the *Liverpool Courier*, December, 1906:

> It is with a shock that one sees such names as Mary Chung or Norman Sing...It is the ambition of a Chinaman in this country to mate with an English girl, and his Oriental wit and passion is directed to this end...the propagation of half-bred Chinese and English in Liverpool is not a matter to be treated lightly...As a rule the son of Chinese and English parents is very low down in the scale of morality. Such a degraded type should not be allowed to grow up in our midst to be a source of contamination and further degradation for generations ahead.[10]

From the Chief Constable of Birkenhead, 1906, however, we get a factual picture:

> The police find the resident Chinamen quiet, inoffensive and industrious people, and although inquiry has been made from time to time, there is no evidence to show that their morals are any worse than those of the rest of the community.[11]

And according to the Chief Constable of Liverpool, 1906:

> The Chinamen have no difficulty in getting English women to marry them or cohabit with them...in all their relations they treat their women well, they are sober and they do not beat their wives.'[12]

In 1910, Miss Robinson, headmistress of a school in London, raised a complaint alleging that Chinese men were cohabiting with teenage girls. This led to an investigation into relationships between Chinese men and English girls. Two white women were reported as saying that they were 'treated kindly, that the Chinamen are considerate and very industrious and always sober'; and a detective inspector from the Limehouse district stated that from his experience 'the Chinaman, if he becomes intimate with an English girl, does not lead her into prostitution but prefers to marry her and treat her well'.[13]

WORKSHEET

1. What words best describe (a) the character Fu Manchu, (b) the Chinese in Britain? Choose some words from the text; add some of your own.

    How does the image of the Chinese and Chinatown portrayed in the Fu Manchu stories compare with the real lives of the Chinese in Britain at that time?

2. A *stereotype* may be defined as a false generalisation e.g. all teenagers are irresponsible. A *prejudice* is a view about an individual or group of individuals not based on an examination of the evidence; a judgement made without giving a fair hearing to each individual case. In what way does Fu Manchu represent a stereotype demonstrating racial prejudice?

3. 'The media's treatment of race is limited in theme and negative in content'. Discuss this statement in relation to the Chinese as portrayed by the press, and in literature and film.

4. 'Folk devils...are central to the creation of a 'moral panic'. A 'moral panic' occurs when people fear that the major values and institutions of society are under attack...('Folk devils') are easy to identify, relatively powerless, and it is fairly simple to exaggerate certain aspects of their behaviour so as to make them appear as a threat to society. They become scapegoats, an easy target for the fear and hate of many people in wider society. The media play an important role in whipping up moral panics, identifying folk devils, amplifying their deviance, and providing targets for popular anxieties', (Glover, 1985, in Haralambos (ed.) p.387).

    Discuss this in relation to the experience of the Chinese in Britain. Why does Fu Manchu appear so threatening? What methods and devices are used; what values and institutions are threatened? How influential is the press? What purposes are served by creating 'moral panics'? What are the consequences?

5. At the House of Lords debate on the Film Bill in 1927, Viscount Peel stressed the importance of having for British youth films that will properly present British civilisation and British standards of conduct and life. In what way did the Fu Manchu films meet this criterion? What image of the British is portrayed?

CHAPTER 2

OF OPIUM AND 'COOLIES': SINO-BRITISH RELATIONS IN THE NINETEENTH CENTURY

How did the notion of the 'yellow peril' come about? Why were the Chinese associated with drugs and seen as threatening to swamp Europe? Why were popular Victorian images of the Chinese so distorted?

Britain and China in the era of 'Free Trade'

Until two centuries ago, Europe was the underdeveloped world, in comparison with China and had been so for many centuries. When Marco Polo got to China in the thirteenth century, he found an orderly society with huge prosperous cities on a scale quite unlike anything in Europe. Many of the basic inventions fundamental to the development of modern society came from China: paper, which transformed literature; gunpowder, which transformed warfare; and the compass, which transformed navigation.

Britain in the seventeenth and eighteenth centuries, however, made vast profits from the slave trade, forcibly transporting people from Africa to work in the plantations of the West Indies. This trade gave a massive boost to the economy which, in turn, assisted the Industrial Revolution. Seeking new supplies of cheap raw materials and markets for its manufactured goods, Britain started to explore profit-making opportunities in India and China.

From China, the British East India Company bought silk, tea and porcelain, offering manufactured goods such as textiles and clocks in exchange. However, since their economy was largely self-sufficient, the

2.1. The Grand Canal, Jiangsu Province, 1793

Chinese had no interest in these goods. The British East India Company was forced to pay for the goods it wanted in silver. To ease this drain on its financial reserves, the company began to carry opium from India, which was new to China. Although this trade contravened Chinese law, it escalated rapidly, from 100 tons in 1800 to 2,000 tons in 1837.

> The Celestial Kingdom possesses all things in prolific abundance and lacks no product within its borders. There is therefore no need to import the manufactures of outside barbarians in exchange for our own products.
>
> *The Emperor Qian Long's response to the British Ambassador's appeal to develop trade 1793.*

In England, rapid industrialisation brought with it economic crisis and increasing social tensions and whilst the economic grievances of the people found expression in the Chartist movement which demanded political and human rights, commercial and industrial interests advocated, in the name of free trade, economic expansion overseas.

Resistance to this policy came with the destruction of the opium stocks of the British merchants in Canton by the Emperor's special commissioner,

2.2. An opium warehouse in India belonging to British merchants of the East India Company.

Lin Zexu, in an attempt to cut off the trade which was draining the Chinese economy and ruining the health and morale of the Chinese people.

This act caused an outcry among the merchants of Liverpool, Manchester and London, who called upon the British government to 'take vengeance'. To protect the merchants' interests in the lucrative opium trade, the government sent a fleet carrying 4,000 troops to occupy the major ports in China.

The outbreak of the Opium War coincided with the British government's attempts to contain the Chartist movement at home, imprisoning its leaders and suppressing its organisation. The Chartists and the Chinese government challenged the British government at the same time, and both simultaneously faced its military troops.

In 1842 the Chinese troops, due to their outdated military equipment and lack of experience of modern warfare, were finally defeated. The Chinese government was forced to sign an unequal treaty, ceding Hong Kong and other major ports to Britain. With China's international trade under its control, the British government was not only able to collect vast

---

Views on the opium trade — from East and West

Is there any single article from China which has done harm to foreign countries? Take tea for example: foreign countries cannot get along a single day without it. If China cuts off this benefit with no sympathy for those who suffer, then what can the barbarians rely upon to keep themselves alive?...On the other hand, articles coming from outside China can only be used as toys. We can take them or get along without them...There is however a class of treacherous barbarians who manufacture opium, smuggle it for sale, and deceive our foolish people, in order to injure their bodies and derive profit therefrom...Such behaviour is repugnant to the feelings of human beings...

...I now give you assurance that we mean to cut off this harmful drug forever. What is forbidden to consume, your dependencies must be forbidden to manufacture...You will be showing that you understand the principle of Heaven by respectful obedience to our commands.

Commissioner Lin Zexu to Queen Victoria, 1839.[1]

The moral obligation of commercial intercourse between nations is founded entirely, exclusively, upon the Christian precept to love your neighbour as yourself...But China, not being a Christian nation, admits no obligation to hold commercial intercourse with others...It is time that this enormous outrage upon the rights of human nature...should cease.

John Quincy Adams on China's refusal to buy opium.[2]

According to the Chartists' newspaper, *The Charter,* of January 12th, 1840, China was:

...destined to destruction by the horrors of civilised warfare for refusing to be poisoned by opium. We doubt the morality of this, and we tell these journalists who prate about National Honour that the working classes of this country will no longer lend themselves to a system of commerce which is supported in such a manner...They no longer believe...that war makes good for trade...[3]

sums in customs duties but was in a position to open up the Chinese market to its manufactured goods. This was regarded as a great victory for free trade. But the Chartists, who had sided with the Chinese, condemned the opium traffic, comparing the Opium War to the unequal struggle between the unarmed working class of Manchester and the British yeomanry at Peterloo.

> It is supreme nonsense to talk as if we were bound to the Chinese by the same rules which regulate international relations in Europe.
>
> *The Duke of Argyll, 1859.*[5]
>
> ---
>
> Never did a division march with a better will to perform a more just and loudly called for act of retribution upon an imperious, treacherous and cruel power.
>
> *The Rev. M'Ghee on the destruction of the Emperor's Summer Palace by British troops in 1860.*[6]

2.3. Lord Elgin is carried in state into Peking after the defeat of China in the second Opium War. He ordered the destruction of the Emperor's Summer Palace.

The Taiping Rebellion

With the loss of customs revenue, and with huge indemnities to pay to the British for the Opium War, the Chinese government increased the tax burden on the peasantry to intolerable levels. The Taiping Rebellion (1851-1862) was the largest popular movement of the nineteenth century. Demanding justice and equal land distribution, the Taiping armies gained control over more than half of China's provinces and endeavoured to introduce a system of progressive government. Their programme aimed to give every person sufficient land to live; to develop water and rail communications; control floods and organise famine relief; abolish concubinage and footbinding; ban opium and make gambling punishable. The Taipings maintained a disciplined army, which included battalions of women, and which took from the rich to distribute to the poor.

Between 1857 and 1860, Britain unleashed a second opium war on the Chinese government and through victory gained further concessions and indemnities. Weakened by this second defeat, the Chinese government lost centralised control over its armed forces.

Reports from missionaries made claims of havoc, mass murder and desolation under the Taipings and the task of defeating the peasant armies fell to a British officer, Captain Gordon, later known as 'Gordon of Khartoum', who took charge of the Emperor's forces, equipped them with modern Western munitions and succeeded in upholding the weakened and increasingly corrupt imperial government, by massive slaughter of the rebels.

Augustus Lindley, chief mate on a British steamer, supported the Taipings and fought with their army. He wrote:

> Much has been stated about the desolating and ruthless character of the Taipings, but I entirely deny the accusation. I have never found them to act with the barbarity that marred the late American war, or act as Englishmen have done to the unfortunate natives of New Zealand...the Taiping army observed strict discipline...[4]

2.4. Britain's persuasive sales technique

The 'Coolie Trade'[7]

With the defeat of the Taipings, the Chinese peasantry faced increasingly exorbitant taxes, which in large part went to pay the indemnities to the British for the second Opium War. The financially weakened Chinese government was unable to maintain the system of flood control and famine relief, and as this system fell progressively into disrepair during the 1870s, the countryside began to suffer regular and massive floods and famines.

As luxury goods entered China from Europe, the landlords, in order to be able to afford a westernised life-style raised rents so that their tenant farmers had to pay up to 70% or 80% of the crop. For many millions of poor peasants the only means of survival was migration.

The Unequal Treaties which concluded the Opium Wars ensured the outflow of cheap goods from China, as well as labour. Under the 1860 Convention, Chinese labourers were allowed to be recruited for work. British agents organised the movement of Chinese labour to British colonies, known as the 'coolie trade'.

> The flood waters crest to the heavens,
> For nine of ten years there have been drowning floods.
> Sons are sold in exchange for a handful of millet;
> Daughters are sold to pay taxes;
> The oxen have starved; the dogs have been slaughtered;
> It's time to swing a bag and go wandering for food.
>
> *Song of poor peasants from Northern China.*[8]

2.5. Chinese labourers at work building the Central Pacific Railroad

Chinese indentured (contract) labour was recruited to work on British-owned plantations in the West Indies and Malaysia, and in the gold mines of South Africa, under conditions little better than slavery.

Chinese labour was also recruited on a large scale to build railroads across the United States, Canada, Australia and New Zealand.

The 'Coolie Traffic'

> By their deaths, though there may be a loss of profit, there can be none of capital for the shipper. The men cost nothing and the more (he) can cram into his vessel the greater must be his profit. It would be a better speculation for the trader, whose junk could only carry properly 300 men, to take on board 600 and lose 250...than it would be for him to start with his legitimate number and land them all safely, for in the first case he would bring 350 men and in the other only 300.

A report on the transportation of Chinese labourers to Malaysia.[9]

In 1874, it was estimated that there had been 34 tragedies in 25 years, including 15 on British ships, whilst the boarding of the other ships was carried out under government inspection in the British-controlled Chinese ports. One such tragedy in 1872 involved the Don Juan, which left Macao with 640 'coolies' on board:

> In mid-ocean, the ship caught fire and the captain and crew abandoned her. Only a few coolies were on deck and they were mostly in chains. The iron gratings on the hatches were locked, and the keys could not be found. When the wretched crowd below burst open the forehatch, it was too late and all but fifty perished.[10]

The 'Coolie Trade' — some figures:

1870	35,000 labourers in San Francisco
1877	17,000 labourers in New South Wales
1906	50,000 labourers in the Rand, the gold reef of South Africa

To organise the 'coolie trade' the British used local mercenaries and brokers. Recruitment was often by deceit, and the conditions of transportation were horrific: many of the 'coolie' ships were perilously overcrowded and mortality was high.

Victorian images of the Chinese

The opium trade continued throughout the nineteenth and early twentieth century, although it was soon overtaken in volume by cotton. In Britain, opposition to the opium traffic also persisted but from quite a different

2.6. A Victorian representation of an opium den in East London

quarter to the now-defeated Chartists, as concern was raised about the spread of the opium habit amongst the British population.

The opium den of East London as a haunt of evil, with its cunning and artful Chinese proprietor wreathed in opium fumes, became a notorious public image in the 1870s.

To those involved in the anti-opium movement, many of whom were missionaries, the Chinese were 'helpless, docile slaves' to be 'saved'. The 'weak and unmanly' nature of the Chinese opium-smoker was emphasised. As if to convince themselves of their superiority as bearers of civilisation, to justify what the British had done, the spread of the opium habit amongst the Chinese was explained in terms of their inferiority and degeneracy. At the same time, the dangers of this 'Chinese' drug to the prime of British society were stressed.

> Very many of these celestials and Indians are mentally and physically inferior, and they go on smoking year after year and seem not very much the worst for it. It is your finer natures that suffer, deteriorate and collapse. For these, great and terrible is the ruin.[11]

Although the popular Victorian press focused on the East End opium dens as a corrupting blight in their midst, one visitor to Chinatown found only thirteen boarding houses and less than half a dozen so-called 'dens':

> they seem to me to be poorly fitted social clubs, and certainly as free from anything visibly objectionable, as to say the least of it, public houses of the same class.[12]

As Chinese emigration grew, the press started forecasting a 'yellow peril'. For their part the Chinese had reason to emigrate, and the development of steam navigation in the 1870s was lowering the cost of bringing cheap labour from afar, so that it was possible to transport the Chinese 'at fabulously low prices to all parts of the world'. Arguing that the isolation of China was a thing of the past, the *Times* warned in 1878 that:

> We shall see the rise in the cities of Europe Chinese quarters which will cause discontent among our working classes, with whom they will have to seriously reckon, and the Chinese will end by fixing themselves among us like Jews.[13]

In 1873, when the Ebbw Vale company threatened to import cheap Chinese labour to break a strike of miners, the *Times* welcomed the entrance of the Chinese people into the labour market of the world: 'They have always been hard-working, patient and economical.' Chinese labour, perceived as docile, came to be associated with cheap labour:

> ...when white men make exorbitant demands for wages, when they begin striking...their employer may be glad that he is not absolutely dependent on them, and that he has at hand a more docile race of beings.[14]

WORKSHEET

1. What words would you use to describe (a) the British, (b) the Chinese *before* having read this chapter and *after*?

    > civilised; over-populated; poverty-stricken; powerful; violent; Christian; uncivilised; backward; wealthy; powerless; barbaric; peaceful; weak; law-abiding; cruel; just; imperious; intelligent; treacherous; superior; unstable; strong; lawless; heathen; stable; greedy; advanced; ignorant; dominating; ruthless; quiescent.

    What changes have you made, and why?

2. Compare and discuss the views of the opium trade held by the Chinese, the Chartists and the British free-traders (see page 16). In what ways did their views of human morality differ? What were the reasons for these differing outlooks?

3. Colonialism has been described as the pursuit of wealth at the expense of the people. In what ways does this apply to British policy towards China?

4. Identify the various links between Britain and China. What were the positive and negative aspects of Sino-British relations?

5. Outline the factors that led to the 'coolie trade'. Explain the reasons for emigration — why was Chinese labour cheap?

    Between 1830 and 1930 the world's population doubled from 1 to 2 billion; between 1840 and 1947, China's population grew by an estimated 42 million, a rate of less than 10%. Between 1830 and 1930, the population of the USA grew from 13 million to 122 million — mostly European immigrants. In what way did the Chinese constitute a 'yellow peril', if at all?

6. What quotations and/or incidents best describe the relations between the Chartists, the Chinese government, the British merchants and the British government?

7. Compare the images of the Chinese portrayed in Victorian times with those of Fu Manchu. Do they evoke similar or different emotions?

    In Victorian times, the Chinese were portrayed as either docile or barbaric. Why do you think they were portrayed in these opposite ways? What were the underlying attitudes and how do these compare with the attitudes of the Chartists?

CHAPTER 3

RACE RIOTS AND REVOLUTION: RELATIONS BETWEEN BRITAIN AND CHINA IN THE EARLY TWENTIETH CENTURY

Why was the idea of the 'yellow peril' so persistent? How entrenched was it? What conditions made possible a positive view of, and response to, the Chinese?

Imperialism and its mounting tensions

For British politicians, financiers and industrialists, faced with the recurring cycle of economic depression and the social tensions which gave rise to mass trade unionism in the 1880s and 1890s, the continued expansion of the Empire was a 'bread and butter' issue, a way to increase exploitation abroad to ease pressures at home. From the early twentieth century, the trend was towards the export of capital, building factories overseas where cheap labour could be employed at source.

With China carved up into different spheres of influence by the European powers, which propped up the decaying and compliant Imperial state, foreign capital flowed in freely to exploit Chinese labour. However, the history of the first half of the twentieth century is also the history of China's struggle for independence from foreign domination and the development of the national movement, initially led by Sun Yatsen, who sought to improve the livelihood of the workers and peasants. But whilst the Chinese people were beginning to organise against the political and economic domination of the British and other European powers to the

> I think we shall have to take the Chinese in hand and regulate them... I believe in the ultimate partition of China — I mean ultimate. The Aryan stock is bound to triumph.'
>
> *Winston Churchill in an interview, 1901, following the antiforeign Boxer rebellion.*[1]

> China is the China of the Chinese. The government of the Chinese should be in the hands of the Chinese... we must restore our national state.
>
> *Sun Yatsen at the founding of the Chinese Revolutionary Alliance (Tong meng hui), 1905.*

point of military confrontation, tensions against Chinese labour mounted among the working class in Britain.

The so-called docility of the Chinese, that is, their acceptance of wages that were lower than those paid to European workers, was causing resentment. In 1898, the TUC praised the US labour unions for their opposition to Chinese immigration, as representing the 'defence of white labour'. When the first immigration legislation was introduced in Britain — the Aliens Restriction Act of 1905 — the 'yellow peril' was a major issue. Thousands of Chinese labourers were being transported to work in the gold mines of South Africa, then a British Colony. Opposition to Chinese indentured labour was an important factor in the defeat of the Conservatives and the victory of the first Liberal government. The TUC declared that the mine owners and Tories were together 'preventing South Africa becoming a white man's country'. Although the TUC criticised the use of Chinese labour as contrary to the traditions of anti-slavery, they argued also that South African jobs should be preserved for white workers.

This then is the colonial scenario that underlay the panic in the Liverpool press at the time. It was at this time of popular hostility against the Chinese, with pressure from certain MPs to compel shipping companies to engage British-only crews, that Rohmer launched his Fu Manchu thrillers, with their warnings of the 'yellow peril'.

3.1. Dr. Sun Yatsen

Chinese and British seamen in conflict

Chinese seamen were recruited in China at very low wages. Signing on a ship at a British port, they got better pay but were regarded by British seamen as competition. Holt's Blue Funnel Line found ways round the immigration controls to recruit Chinese seamen, and in 1908 used them to break a strike in London. There were ugly scenes as the Chinese, under police escort, passed through the crowds of strikers to board the British ships. Whilst the Chinese formed their own union to improve their conditions, the British seamen's unions called for tighter immigration controls and their journals kept up a continual, hostile attack: 'You know, we know and they know, that the Chinaman isn't worth a toss as a seaman; that his only claim to indulgence is that he is cheap.'[2] During the seamen's strike of 1911, the Chinese were again used as strike breakers, and hostility among the British was whipped up by the seamen's leader, the so-called 'Captain' Tupper. After five weeks of striking, all Cardiff's thirty or so Chinese laundries were attacked and wrecked in a night of violence.

But the year 1911 was significant also for quite another reason: the October Revolution in China. It established a Republic with Sun Yatsen as president, in the face of British, US and Japanese warships. Not many months before Rohmer was speculating about an international Chinese conspiracy, Sun Yatsen had been in London securing the financial support of the Chinese community to set up a republic. This first Republic was, however, to prove unstable and short-lived.

Britain's double dealings

Chinese labour was again used by the British government on a large scale in the First World War, when a labour corps of 96,000 was recruited from Shandong province. In 1916, Britain was in danger of losing the war because of the shortage of shipping and delays in supplies: the solution was to use Chinese labour in the docks and railway yards of France, thus releasing more British workers to be recruited into the army.

Although recruited on the assurance that they would not be soldiers nor involved in fighting, the Chinese were subject to harsh military discipline. Over 2,000 lost their lives, many in aerial attacks on munitions stores. Although they worked behind the lines, their lives were endangered, yet they received only one penny a day in pay as compared with the British pay of one shilling (twelve pence).

China was at first neutral in the World War. Then they began to support the Allies, in the expectation that with Germany's defeat, the concessions that Germany controlled in China would be returned to the Chinese. What the Chinese government did not know was that whilst the British were

A British officer commented as follows on the Chinese Labour Corps in France:

> ...they are only great big boys, and whatever their age may be, they are none of them older than ten years in character — very amenable, easily managed with kindness and firmness and are loyal to the core, if treated with consideration...A dog is the same.[3]

recruiting Chinese labour to enhance their own war aims, they had concluded a secret pact with the Japanese to support Japan's claims to Germany's Chinese territories.

At the Versailles Peace Conference in 1919, while the Chinese Labour Corps was still at work in France cleaning up the battlefields and burying the Allied dead, the Allies upheld Japan's claims to Chinese territory.

This was met with anger and indignation by people across China. On May 4th, students gathered in protest in Peking and encountered troops and British police sent to crush their demonstration. The arrest of many students led to mass strikes and further demonstrations by students and

3.2. A contingent of the Chinese Labour Corps

3.3. May 4th movement protests, 1919

workers across China, which continued into the 1920s. The formation of the Chinese Communist Party in 1921 was a part of this momentum of popular activism and in many ways the May 4th movement of 1919 presaged the Chinese revolution of 1949.

The divisive role of racism

With the end of the First World War, Britain faced social unrest across its Empire and throughout its spheres of influence. There were mass protests in China, constitutional agitation in India and political unrest in several African colonies. There was also deep trouble at its very heart. According to social historian Allen Hutt, 1919 saw 'the most...stormy age of profound social crisis ever known by this country and that overwhelming majority of its people who toil to live'.[4]

In Glasgow, a strikers' demonstration was attacked by police and its leaders beaten; miners and railway and transport workers were in a highly militant mood and there was a lightning police strike. There were soldiers' strikes and mutinies in army camps and depots and thousands of Army Service Corps men commandeered lorries and poured into London to lay their grievances before the government, as demobilised soldiers faced unemployment.

But in the summer, the unrest degenerated into race riots, particularly in the ports of Liverpool and Cardiff, where black and Asian seamen who had assisted the British government in its war effort were now in direct competition with the demobilised whites for jobs. The popular press played on fears of sexual competition, with stories of the black man — 'part savage, part animal' — and their women 'with no self-respect'. White workers were mobilised into lynch mobs and armed gangs attacked black workers.

On June 17th, the *Star* newspaper printed a report claiming that the Chinese had benefited from the war by seizing the jobs of Englishmen fighting at the front, by overflowing from their 'original quarter' and by forming alliances with white women. The following day in Poplar, a gang attacked a house occupied by a Chinese family, cleared out all the furniture, stacked it in the middle of the street and set fire to it, causing a huge blaze that gutted the house.

As Peter Fryer (1984) points out:

> The divisive role of racism in Liverpool and Cardiff that year is obvious... This was very far from the revolution that Britain's rulers feared and Glasgow strike leaders admitted they should have been aiming for.[5]

The Billie Carlton Case: a question of 'moral panic'

In the months before these racial attacks the popular press had been filled with stories of drug trafficking in Chinatown. In November 1918, a popular young showgirl, Billie Carlton, was found dead in her London flat. It was thought that she had died of a cocaine overdose, supposedly from a Chinese source in Limehouse. The police began an investigation which was to point to American as much as Chinese involvement, but it was the Chinese connection that attracted public attention. A continuous stream of stories about Chinatown appeared in the press.

The story was seized upon by Sax Rohmer, who saw it as a 'public duty' to write another book focusing on the traffickers. His novel, *Dope*, sensationalised the Carlton case, helping to create the classic myth of drug abuse — a beautiful young girl, a malevolent male supplier with a sexual interest in the victim, a Chinese source of drugs and a setting that alternated between West End drawing rooms and squalid Limehouse dives.

In 1920, the film *The Yellow Claw* based on the novel *Dope* was released. Purporting to be a study of drug traffic, it portrays the Chinese 'underworld' of the East End with an accentuated eeriness — scenes of a labyrinthine opium den, a lurking shadow of an elusive Chinaman, a yellow claw-like hand appearing mysteriously through the apertures in walls and between curtains.

3.4. *The Yellow Claw*

All this provided the background for the introduction in September 1920 of the Dangerous Drugs Act. Following the race riots and the setting up of reparation committees, a further Aliens Restriction Act was passed in 1919, again with the support of the seamen's unions, calling for immigration control of the Chinese. But it was following the Dangerous Drugs Act that the most damage was inflicted on the Chinese in Britain. From October there were continual police raids on Chinatown and people were arrested not only for mere possession but also for gambling. Apparently the Chinese liked to play a game called 'puk-a-pu', similar to the game of 'House' (which was permitted in the British Army in France).

An incessant flow of Chinese people appeared at magistrates courts daily, and a number were deported.

From October, the press was filled with headlines such as 'The Lure of the Yellow Man', or 'Chinatown Scandal'. This precipitated a flood of letters from the public declaring that these 'outrages' should no longer be tolerated. Once again, fears of sex and of drugs were linked: the scare was that Chinese men doped young girls with sweets in the course of converting 'these slips of growing white womanhood' into the 'slaves of laundry lords'.

Further reports featured an interview with an out-of-work tailoress who, having won some money gambling in Chinatown, returned there with her friends; an interview with a Chinese man who objected to deportations as unfair on grounds that 'there are plenty of English in China';

Running a story on the 'movement of girls from the West End to East London', the *London Evening News* reported:

> Part of the problem is the youth of the girls; it is obvious that they do not appreciate the significance of what they are doing, and the difficulty is to restrain them. It is of common occurrence that these girls... are lured by some fatal fascination to the underworld.

> Drugs, gambling and appeals to every human passion have their place in Limehouse. It is the distributing centre for opium and cocaine...

> ...a detective-sergeant made reference in court to the numbers of half-caste children...English girls are giving birth to children the fathers of whom are Arabs, Chinese, Japanese and Negroes.

> The ordinary machinery of the law is unequal to this new problem...The time has come to draw a cordon round this area of London and forbid any white woman from frequenting it.

'The Lure of the Yellow Man' *The London Evening News*, Oct. 4th, 1929.

---

reference to the problems of ex-soldiers and respectable workers in the East End who could not find houses because 'Chinamen were buying the property'; and a comment from 'Captain' Tupper that Limehouse was the 'overseas headquarters of China'.

In 1922, the film *Cocaine* was advertised with posters showing a leering Chinaman. It attracted large audiences throughout the country and provoked a protest to the Home Office from the Chinese community.

Arrests continued to the late 1920s in towns with Chinese communities. Liverpool's Chinese quarter, noted at the turn of the century as a 'transformed area', was reported by 1927 to have 'a dying atmosphere'.

The irony was that for most of this period British manufacturers were still involved in smuggling a large part of their opiate products to China, in violation of both Chinese and international laws.

The tide begins to turn

Following the May 4th Movement, Chinese workers and students became more organised. A strike-wave involving over a quarter of a million workers for some eighteen months started in Hong Kong in 1922 with a seamen's strike over pay. They received only one fifth of the wages of

3.5. Victims of famine, July 1930

The British American Tobacco Company extracted a surplus from the peasant economy of Shandong...the company reinvested only 7% of its profits between 1913 and 1941. To induce the peasants to grow the needed 'bright tobacco', BAT provided seeds and guarantees of purchase in the early years only to withdraw those subsidies in the1920s during the price wars to force out its Chinese competitors, the Nanyang Brothers...The company's rate of profit in China (about 17% of sales) was much higher than could be obtained in the US — once involved, the peasants were locked into a relation of dependency.

Philip Huang, The Peasant Economy and Social Change in North China *(1985), p.130.*

foreign seamen. Since many of the companies employing Chinese labour and investing in China were foreign-owned, these strikes were directed essentially against foreign capital.

This massive labour protest could not fail to attract the attention of the TUC, which in 1924 called for an inquiry into the condition of workers in the East. Reports were to show conditions reminiscent of the earliest days of the Industrial Revolution in Britain, above all in the foreign-owned textile mills, where adults worked 16 hours a day, young children worked at the age of five and infants slept on filthy floors whilst their mothers worked for starvation wages.

In 1925, there were more strikes in Shanghai. Students joined the strikers, demanding the recovery of foreign concessions. More than 10,000 people rallied in front of the British police headquarters on May 30th, shouting 'Down with Imperialism'. The British police opened fire, killing and wounding many.

Mass protests over this incident developed into a revolutionary movement, led by Sun Yatsen's party, the *Guomindang*. Meanwhile in Britain the TUC Congress condemned the use of British armed forces as strike-breakers and passed a resolution to put a stop to these 'murderous crimes'. The Labour Party Conference also registered its protest and called on the government to revise the Unequal Treaties through which Britain had taken control of concessions in China.

Throughout the 1926 General Strike in Britain, the most important international campaign was the 'Hands Off China' movement. It was supported by trades councils and unions and continued to organise for months after the strike itself was defeated. The *Guomindang* armies, preparing to launch their Northern Expedition to establish an independent republic of China, sent their greetings to the miners on strike in Britain.

Although the *Guomindang* succeeded in establishing its capital in Wuhan, taking over the British concessions in that city, the Chinese revolution was to take many twists and turns before the People's Republic was established in 1949. Nevertheless, the events of 1926/7 represented in many ways a defeat for the British government. Although British warships continued to patrol the rivers and seas of China, the policies had provoked such anti-British hostility in China that they had to be changed. Britain in effect became a secondary power among other foreign powers, particularly Japan and the US which sought to become the dominant influence in China.

International Solidarity

In 1925 the Scarborough TUC Congress passed a resolution:

> ...with a view to doing everything possible to put a stop to the murderous crimes being perpetrated against our working class comrades who are struggling to improve their horrible working conditions.

It condemned:

> ...the use of British armed forces as strike-breakers in the interests of the gang of unscrupulous capitalists and imperialists who are exploiting the lives of men, women and even children of a tender age in China at the present time, and insists on their immediate withdrawal.

The Liverpool Labour Party Conference in 1925 called on the government to:

> ...treat the Chinese people as a Sovereign State responsible for their own government: to enter freely into negotiations with that government for the revision of all Treaties imposed on them...

> The implications of the sweated labour of the East for the conditions of the British workers are at last beginning to penetrate the slowly moving perceptions of Labour politicians. The imperialism which seemed to offer such munificent rewards to a patriotic labour movement is a two edged sword: it can give, but it can also destroy. The most ardent visions of a national 'British' socialism...vanish into thin air when it is realised that British capital is busily developing the exploitation of low paid...Asiatic labour in order from that (nationally) impregnable basis to undermine the economic foundations of the British working class.

R. Palme Dutt, Notes of the Month, Labour Monthly, May1925.

WORKSHEET

1. From the illustrations and quotations accompanying this chapter, pick two contrasting images and comments. Discuss the reasons for your choice.

2. Identify the reasons for Chinese hostility towards British policies and actions. Were their feelings justified?

3. Stuart Hall *et al.* (1978) identify the different stages in a 'moral panic' as social instability, values threatened by anti-social acts, media use of the story, headlines 'labelling' a group as bad, exaggeration of the initial story to attract interest, moral panic, responses including calls to strengthen law and order, increased policing and harassment.

   In what way does the case of Billie Carlton fit these stages? Are there any elements that do not apply, and if not, why not?

4. Peter Fryer argues that to understand the race riots of 1919 we must see them in the light of the social unrest that existed in Britain at that time.

   Do you think that racism towards the Chinese has its roots in the conditions of economic instability and crisis in Britain or in the history of Britain's relations with China? Give reasons for your answer.

   Why did the Chinese, victims of the opium traffic, become identified as drug traffickers undermining British society?

5. How would you compare the two incidents of strike-breaking in 1911 by Chinese seamen in Britain and 1925 by British troops in China, and the responses to them?

6. In the light of the comment by Palme Dutt on page 35, discuss what had changed in the attitudes of British Trade Unions and workers in 1911 and 1919, and in 1926. What conclusions would you draw from this about conflict between British and Chinese people?

7. Look again as Viscount Peel's contribution to the House of Lords debate on the Film Bill of 1927 in the worksheet for Chapter 1. What significance would you attach to his view? To what extent can the character Fu Manchu be described as epitomising the rising tide of Asian politics?

   What difference does it make to view what was going on in Britain in an international context?

CHAPTER 4

THE CHINESE IN BRITAIN TODAY: MEDIA IMAGES AND REAL LIVES

How and why has the myth of the 'yellow peril' been kept alive in Britain? What are the consequences for the Chinese who live in Britain?

The Chinese in film: from Bruce Lee to Mutant Turtles

Along with 'chicken chop suey' and 'sweet and sour pork', the Oriental martial arts are among the few things foreign to become part of Western culture. Kung Fu films have become such a vogue that nowadays it is almost compulsory for any streetwise screen hero to demonstrate his 'machismo' with a show of prowess in one of the forms of Oriental fighting.

Weak in plot and characterisation, these films aim to capture the public's imagination with a mixture of dramatic fight scenes and pseudo-Eastern mysticism which play upon popular notions of the mysterious powers of the exotic East. Featuring things Chinese generally spells drama in the form of drugs, street crime, sinister international syndicates and gang warfare of unprecedented violence. The Chinese appear as outsiders, evil-doers, bound by tradition beyond law and order, or at best as ageing representatives of an ancient warrior code of honour, mouthing fortune-cookie platitudes. They inhabit mysterious lands and urban ghettos — the underworld or, in the case of Splinter the Rat, the sewers, as if to stress the gulf between East and West.

Rarely do Asian actors appear in a starring role — except in the case of Bruce Lee. But from *Enter the Dragon* to *Teenage Mutant Ninja Turtles*, the good guys, whether yellow or white, are those that rush to the aid of the

4.1. The Kung Fu genre has spawned a growing sub-culture of videos, shops, clothing and all the paraphenalia of training kits.

West or to the protection of a white damsel-in-distress, against the threat of ultimate villainy — the sinister forces of the Orient that threaten to engulf all in a wave of violence and drugs.

Innocent, comic-strip stuff? Harmless fun? Chinese characters are generally used in film to represent the ultimate in evil, the better to highlight the superiority of Western civilisation, whose law and order is upheld under the leadership of the white hero.

The Year of The Dragon (1985)

> Supergripping, stunningly-staged Chinese mafia movie...starring Michael Rourke as a Polack cop — tough, incorruptible and relentless in his pursuit of criminals. When a prominent business-man/mob leader in New York's Chinatown is assassinated by a Chinese youth gang, Rourke is assigned to Chinatown to clean up the gang problem, but the problems go much deeper...the teenage hoodlums are under the control of an ambitious heroin kingpin...

Directed by Michael Cimino, with screenplay by Oliver Stone, this film about the Triads portrays Chinatown as the sinister headquarters of an international conspiracy buttressing popular images of the Chinese as barbaric, exploitative, in-fighting. The film drew protest from Chinese communities from New York to London and Manchester.

> Given that few Chinese films are screened in the West, the *Year of the Dragon...* will create a pit in many Western people's minds where all other things Chinese will subsequently be put. Millions will watch it. What is simply Chinese will suffer by association...

SiYu bilingual magazine editorial No.10 March 1986

The Chinese Community....

Size:	200,000 approximately
Places of Origin:	Hong Kong, especially the New Territories, Malaysia, Singapore, China.
Main Occupation:	Catering

4.2. Chinese protest outside Manchester cinema screening of *Year of the Dragon* — 'Must we suffer this?'

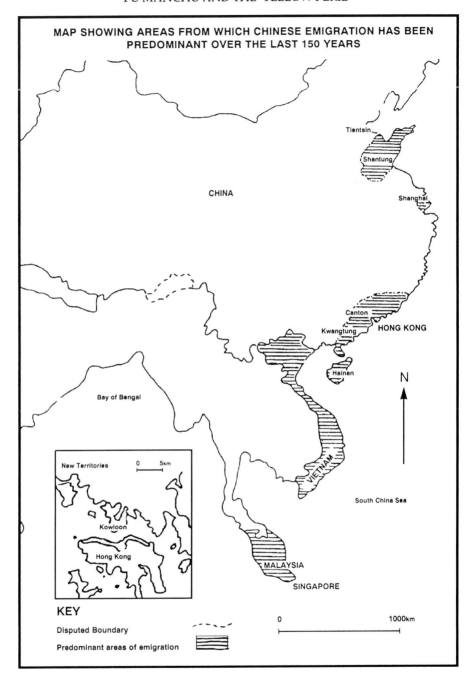

MAP SHOWING AREAS FROM WHICH CHINESE EMIGRATION HAS BEEN
PREDOMINANT OVER THE LAST 150 YEARS

4.3. Map

...in the chip shop

The Chinese in Britain form a community of significant size yet they are virtually ignored. Unlike other ethnic minorities, they are scattered throughout Britain, working in restaurants and take-aways all over the country. The growth in the catering trade in the 1960s and 1970s drew Chinese migrants, especially from Hong Kong, where most had a family farming background. Running restaurants and chip shops suited their experience in family enterprise and required only small amounts of capital and limited English vocabulary. Most were only able to come to Britain under the voucher system, provided under the Commonwealth Immigration Act 1962. Since this system of immigration control required the employer to apply for a voucher on the worker's behalf, these rules tended to reinforce the concentration of Chinese in catering, as friends and relatives arranged employment for their fellow villagers.

Even those who are born and go to school in Britain still end up in catering: according to a recent report this is largely owing to the failure of the education system to equip Chinese pupils with a wide range of skills.[1]

4.4. 'With only a machine for company'

Work in catering is hard and tedious, involving long and anti- social hours which together with the barriers of language, mean social isolation for many.

The Chinese traditionally overcome difficulties through self- reliance and mutual aid: in major cities like London, Manchester and Liverpool, Chinatowns have developed with supermarkets growing in number to supply the specialist needs of the restaurants and take-aways, wholesaler and import traders, and other services to support the community, such as advice centres, solicitors, Chinese doctors, social clubs and schools to teach young Chinese their mother-tongue.

...in the press

Other people know little about the Chinese community in Britain. Although many have regular contact over the counter of the chip shop, this contact is limited and their views remain limited. The Chinese appear in the press only if there is something sensational...a fight, choppers, drugs. Mention the Triads, and what springs to mind? Gambling, vice, extortion — an underworld of drugs and crime lurking in the dark alleyways of Chinatown. 'Arch-criminals of Chinatown'; 'War Alert as Triad Army marches in'; 'Triad gang scare hits Brum streets' — these are typical headlines, generally based on little evidence, but which sensationalise and criminalise the Chinese communities.

'Triad Terror at Your Chinese Take away: Evil Gangs have links with nearly all Oriental businesses in Britain'

Under this headline, the *Sunday People* ran an article (6/11/88) which, without citing any evidence, asserted that '90% of Chinese businesses are somehow connected with the Triads'. The paper apparently wanted its readers to believe that a Triad boss lurked behind the counter of every Chinese take-away in the country.

Martin Booth, author of a recent book *The Triads*, is another writer who appears intent on exposing these alleged 'professional gangsters' as being involved in 'international conspiracy' operating from within the 'supposedly quiet and law-abiding Chinese community'.

The fact that throughout the 1980s there were only two murders and one arrest related to Triad activities in Britain did not deter Booth from asserting that the Triads control so many aspects of life in the Chinese community that young people find it hard to get employment without Triad membership. According to Booth, the Triads run many legitimate businesses — shops and restaurants — as well as their numerous illegal activities: protection rackets, loan sharking and above all, drugs — with immigration rackets providing a source for drug smuggling. Having alleged widespread membership of Triad gangs among Chinese youth, and of the connection between legitimate and illegitimate activities, Booth links the Chinese and their chip shops into an world-wide network of thuggery, drugs and conspiracy, which dodges round immigration controls and hides behind impenetrable cultural traditions.

Extortion... gambling... prostitution... fraud... corruption... and above all drugs: the criminal activities of the Triads are vast and now pose possibly the biggest single threat to international law enforcement agencies.

Wherever there is a Chinese community, Triad criminals enjoy a lucrative parasitical living by 'squeezing' its members. For thousands of Chinese this is bad enough. But now with the imminent handover of Hong Kong to China in 1997, the Triads are on the move. America, Australia, Canada, Holland and the UK are all in the front line, and now the street thugs wielding meat cleavers are operating alongside a new generation of Triad techno-criminals, skilled in money laundering techniques and able to manipulate stock market movements and infiltrate computerised banking systems.

Bound by blood ties, secret rituals and fearsome oath-takings, the Triads ruthlessly demand total loyalty from their members and mete out summary and bloody retribution in the form of 'choppings' to those who oppose or betray them... Unlike the Mafia, few people have penetrated their elaborate defences: even fewer have lived to tell the tale.

From the flyleaf of Martin Booth's book: The Triads

Organised crime exists in all societies and communities — the Chinese are no exception. Yet the media exaggerates the Triads out of all proportion, encouraging people to suppose that all take-aways are a front for an international drugs racket, which is today regarded as the most dangerous crime.

Lynn Pan, whose research for her book on the Chinese overseas took her to meet and interview members of Chinese communities in Britain, the US, Australia, Singapore and elsewhere, found that '...most Chinese who live abroad do so in happy ignorance of the existence of Triads and protection rackets'.[2] The Chinese in fact have more to fear from quite other types of criminals.

4.5. Collage of newspaper headings

Racial harassment: the Chinese experience

It is generally believed that the Chinese do not suffer much in the way of racial abuse or attacks. This is not the case. A recent survey[3] of Chinese living in Tameside, Greater Manchester, found that they are vulnerable to racial harassment, particularly abuse but also assault and vandalism, sometimes on a regular basis.

The experience of the owners of a Chinese restaurant in Tilbury which was forced to close down in 1987 after repeated and continual harassment from local youths, is not unusual. A report by the Essex Community Relations Council on this local area of Thurrock found that violent attacks on the staff and property of Asian and Chinese restaurants were 'much more frequent' than attacks on white-owned restaurants.[4]

Explanations as to why racial harassment of the Chinese has been underestimated vary: some argue that the Chinese do not report incidents to the police because of language difficulties and their cultural reluctance to get involved with officialdom. Others talk of police indifference...

Chinese speak out...

At a recent conference to discuss racial attacks in the workplace, on housing estates and in schools, many older members of the community spoke out about their experiences over the last twenty years of racial abuse and attacks and the emotional and psychological stress these caused, and of the indifference of the police to these problems. As one man said:

'It is such a common experience that we did not even talk about it, there seemed to be no solution to it. Talking about it only added to the sense of powerlessness and frustration. What I speak of today is an experience I have not shared for twenty odd years. For the first time I feel that sharing my experience could have some kind of positive effect.'[5]

Eat and run...

When I was working in my elder brother's restaurant, we had about three fights a week...eat-and-run was very frequent. Some people wait until the waiter is busy and run for the exit; some people just stand up and walk very calmly towards the door as if they are saying 'I'm 6' 2" and 15 stone; you're 5' 7" and 9 stone — Try and stop me'. A common trick people try is after they finish most of the meal, they pull a hair out or pick up something from the floor and put it in their meal. They say: 'Look sir, your dish has got some foreign particle in it, I do not wish to continue with the meal...' Some people push the waiters around and go straight out...

Kenneth Lin interviewed by Jamie Kenny in SiYu No.24 February, 1989.

4.6. Campaigning to support the Diamond Four in Chinatown, London

The case of the Diamond Four

When five white customers at the Diamond Chinese restaurant in the West End of London were asked to pay for the meal they had eaten, they set upon the waiter, pushed him to the floor and started to punch and kick him. Three of his colleagues went to his rescue and got involved in a fight. When the police came, they immediately assumed that responsibility lay with the waiters — the white customers were taken to hospital, while the waiters were taken to the police station and charged with affray, wounding with intent and unlawful wounding. At their trial they were convicted of affray and given harsh sentences of two years imprisonment. This happened in 1988.

The Chinese community mobilised a strong campaign, raising £8,000 for the appeal. They succeeded in getting the sentences reduced to nine months. The campaign was supported by Chinese groups all over the country. As the leaflet 'Defend the Diamond 4' said: 'the necessity to defend themselves from racist customers is now an everyday experience for waiters in Chinatown'.[6]

Mr. Richards denied that he and his friends were drunk and rowdy, though admitted each had consumed around six pints of beer before entering the restaurant...the accused waiters claimed that the customers were drunk and abusive: 'They started hitting the tables with their knives and forks and shouting', said Mr. Li. 'I told them there was no spare ribs and he said 'Fucking hell, is this a restaurant'...' said Mr. Lam. Mr. Richards, incidentally works for the diplomatic service. 'You disgraced yourselves, your families and the Chinese community' said the judge on passing sentence.

From 'Foreign Office Man Clubbed by Waiters', The Guardian, 16/6/87

Tebbit steps up war on Chinese Immigration

Racial harassment of the Chinese has continued in an atmosphere of anti-Chinese hostility in the political arena over the issue of immigration from Hong Kong. Originally seized by the British in an attack against China, Hong Kong has been under British colonial government for some 150 years according to the terms of an unequal treaty which leased the island until 1997. Many Hong Kong people, including those who worked in the British administration are anxious about the change of government when the island is returned to China. Upholding its 'duty to offer safe haven for former Crown servants', the government's plan to grant right of abode in Britain to some 50,000 'key personnel' from Hong Kong, sparked off a wave of protest in December, 1989, from Tory backbenchers objecting to this amending of the immigration legislation.

'These islands of ours are already overcrowded... great waves of immigration by people who do not share our culture, our language, our ways of social conduct, in many cases who owe no allegiance to our culture... is a destabilising factor in society...

Most people in Britain do not want to live in a multicultural, multiracial society... It has been foisted on them... the fear is that they will be swamped by people of different culture, history and religion...'

Norman Tebbit.[7]

'We don't want them in. We don't want a single one of them... people are sick to death of massive immigration.'

Tim Janman, Tory MP for Thurrock.

'After ten years of controlling immigration into this country, we would have all the nasties back... All those hideous people...'

A *Tory backbench MP.*[8]

Chinese hit in Ulster racist attack

The Royal Ulster Constabulary has not ruled out racism as the motive for a barbaric gun attack on three Chinese men in Belfast recently.

The attack, which took place in the Jumbo Chinese take-away on the Crumlin Road, was claimed by the UVF. The paramilitary organisation is known to have strong links with right-wing extremists throughout Europe and the UK including the National Front.

Verbal attacks on the Chinese community especially in Belfast have been gaining momentum over the past few years, as right-wing racists try to emulate their counterparts in Britain by substituting Chinese for blacks and Pakistanis.

This has also found its way into politics. David Kerr, one-time Secretary of the Independent Unionist Association, gave a page-long interview in the right-wing paper *Nationalism Today* in which he echoed concern about the growing number of Chinese in North Belfast. 'One thing that has come up is the issue of Chinese restaurants. Over the past few years Chinese restaurants have been mushrooming in almost every street and thoroughfare in Belfast and in provincial towns. In North Belfast in particular there is a whole lot of them and this has caused no end of concern.'

'We in the Independent Unionist Associations have no inhibitions at all about speaking out against this menace.' Kerr then says he is worried about the handover of Hong Kong to China, not through any humanitarian concern but, as he says, this 'could mean we are inundated with a whole lot more Chinese people that we could well do without.'

Searchlight, No. 183, Sept., 1990, p.8.

Employment in restaurants and take-aways means Chinese families are particularly vulnerable to various forms of racial harassment, because of late opening hours and shop front premises. As a scattered community, the Chinese, despite their small number, often serve as a substitute target for aggression against Asians and blacks in predominantly white areas. But the plight of the many Chinese families up and down the country who, when simply trying to earn a living, are forced to abandon their means of livelihood due to the behaviour of certain people in the community in which they live and work, receives little attention in the media.

Instead of such behaviour being checked, racial attacks are carried out in an atmosphere of political hostility towards the Chinese, whilst the media whips up fears of a growing Triad threat. The views and attitudes of politicians and media alike favour increased control over the Chinese and the breakup of their culture.

Reality is turned into its opposite: for 'organised crime of the Triads against international law and order' read the truth of organised crime against the Chinese in Ulster. When the Chinese attempt to defend themselves from racial assault, the police not infrequently charge the victims with criminal affray, while the attackers become witnesses for the prosecution as in the case of the Diamond Four.

The myth of the Chinese as a closed, conspiratorial community master-minded behind the scenes by professionals in organised crime and drugs, orchestrated from Hong Kong, flourishes on the basis of very little evidence. Tebbit, the press and the big screen — whether in thrillers or spoofs — all work on deep-seated images. The idea of a 'yellow peril' threatening to swamp Western civilisation, master-minded by an Oriental super- villain conspiring to overthrow the West in a sinister, underhanded manner, has very deep roots. It is high time these roots were noe torn up.

WORKSHEET

1. The Triads and the Mafia (and the IRA) are often mentioned in the same breath, to heighten the sense of threat. In America, Italian civil rights activists have campaigned against the use of the term 'Mafia' and its replacement with the ethnically neutral term 'organised crime'. They argue that to use the term 'Mafia' distorts the public's view of crime and makes it representative of a special kind of wrong-doing, one that is peculiarly Italian.

    (a) Substitute 'organised crime' for 'Triads' in the headlines on Page 43. What difference does it make?

    (b) What other examples can you think of in which crime is linked to race? Why is the issue of crime often linked to race in this way?

2. 'He (Tebbit) seems to be playing into the hands of Enoch Powell- style racist people who need to be checked not encouraged'. President of the Bradford Council of Mosques.

    (a) Examine the quotes from the Tory MPs on Page 49. What are their implications?

    (b) Argue the case supporting the statement quoted above.

    (c) What message do you think the Tory MP for Thurrock was giving his constituents, who were involved in the racial harassment of the Chinese chippie which was forced to close down?

    (d) How might such behaviour be checked?

3. Examine the images of the Chinese portrayed in film, by the press and by right-wing Tory MPs. How do they compare?

4. 'A... cause of the community's insularity has been its tightly-knit social structure, brought over largely intact from Hong Kong... one... result: the organised crime syndicates known as the Triads'. *The Economist*, April, 28th, 1990.

    'The isolated nature of the Chinese community lies not in inherent cultural traits of the Chinese, but in Britain's attitude towards Chinese immigrants, with Britain's immigration and employment laws which discouraged the Chinese from venturing beyond the the catering business'. Cheung Siu-ming, Chair of the Chinese Information and Advice Centre, London (Tam, 1985).

    Which explanation is the most reasonable and why?
    What are the implications?

5. According to the Metropolitan Police, London, in 1985, 'the Chinese community is not subject to a statistically significant degree of racial abuse and attacks'.

    How would you account for the differing perceptions of the extent and seriousness of racial violence and harassment? Do the police have different interpretations from those of the Chinese community? Does the variance in perception imply that the police are themselves racist and are implicated in attacks on the Chinese community? Or are the Chinese so sceptical of the indifferent attitudes of the police that they just don't bother to report the incidents?

CONSOLIDATION WORKSHEET

1. What image or event would you select as illustrative of an image totally opposite to that of Fu Manchu and why?

2. What can be learnt from this historical appraisal of a racist myth in this book? Which issues are still relevant today?

3. How do you see the relation between immigration legislation and the wider political debates and processes demonstrated in this book? What do you think can be learned from this?

4. What was the impact of the 'yellow peril' on political and economic life in Britain? How do you account for the fact that a numerically insignificant community with no more than an average crime rate became the focus for public attention and often hostility, under scrutiny from the police, media and authorities?

5. What are the ways in which various racial stereotypes seep into our culture? How do you assess the role of the media in creating, reflecting, influencing and exaggerating these stereotypes? Is the media's role to be explained in terms of making money or is it representing powerful vested economic and political interests? Give justifications for your answer.

6. 'Fact and fantasy have a habit of being confused where attitudes to foreigners are concerned'. Discuss in relation to Fu Manchu and the 'yellow peril' and the Chinese. Why should this be the case?

7. Outline the different stand-points within Britain which are for and against colonialism and imperialism? Why do they differ?

8. How would you account for racial prejudice: as concealing and legitimating exploitation by asserting inferiority; as diverting attention from the real economic situation; as used by white workers to protect their position in the labour market? Use examples from this book to illustrate your argument.

9. To what extent is racism part of British culture? Does this mean that all whites are racist? How entrenched is racism, and what would it take to change this?

10. From the quotations supplied below, choose two to compare and contrast in appraising the myth of the 'yellow peril':

> 'Sudden or limited contact between different nations or ethnic groups gives rise, as a rule, to all kinds of popular beliefs. Such beliefs spring from ignorance, fear, and the need to find plausible explanations for perplexing physical and cultural differences... ...ancient myths about Africa and Africans were widely believed (in England in the sixteenth and seventeenth centuries)...Once the English slave trade...had begun to operate...the economic basis had been laid for all those

ancient scraps of myth and prejudice to be woven into a more or less coherent racist ideology: the mythology of race. Race prejudice is scrappy and self-contradictory...Racism is relatively systematic and internally consistent. In time it acquires a pseudo-scientific veneer that glosses over its irrationalities and enables it to claim intellectual respectability. And it is transmitted largely through the printed word. ...The primary functions of race prejudice are cultural and psychological. The primary functions of racism are economic and political.'

Peter Fryer, *Staying Power* (1985), pages 133-5.

'...racism is not... a white problem, but a problem of an exploitative white power structure; power is not something white people are born into, but that which they derive from their position in a complex race/sex/class hierarchy...confusion arises from the wrong use of terms. Racism, strictly speaking, should be used to refer to structures and institutions with power to discriminate. What individuals display is racialism, prejudiced attitudes, which give them no intrinsic power over non-whites. That power is derived from racist laws, constitutional conventions, judicial precedents, institutional practices — all of which have the imprimatur of the state. In a capitalist state, that power is associated with the power of the capitalist class — and racial oppression cannot be disassociated from class exploitation.'

A. Sivanandan, *Race & Class*, Vol. XXVI No. 4, (1985).

'The ordinary English worker hates the Irish worker as a competitor who lowers his standard of life. In relation to the Irish worker he feels himself a member of a ruling nation and so turns himself into a tool of the aristocrats and capitalists of his country against Ireland, thus strengthening their domination over himself. He cherishes religious, social and national prejudice against the Irish worker...

This antagonism is artificially kept alive and intensified by the press, the pulpit, the comic papers... This antagonism is the secret of the impotence of the English working class, despite its organisation. It is the secret by which the capitalist class maintains its power. And that class is fully aware of it.'

Karl Marx, *On Colonialism* (1976), p.337.

'...the current notions of race are an integral part of the history of Western Europe, drawing upon many aspects of that story. These notions cannot be separated from the rest of that history and attributed to single factors like capitalism, colonialism, scientific error or personal prejudice. The sources of popular imagery concerning race are very diverse and the interrelations between their growth and contemporary political affairs is far too complex for the whole historical sequence to be explained in simple terms.'

M. Banton & J. Harwood, *The Race Concept* (1975), p.9.

Notes

Chapter 1
Fu Manchu: the 'Yellow Peril' Incarnate

1. from *The Insidious Dr. Fu Manchu*, quoted in Wu (1982), p.165.
2. quoted in Van Ash (1972), pp.74-5.
3. from *The Mystery of Dr. Fu-Manchu* (1913) quoted in Waller (1985), p.8.
4. ibid.
5. Van Ash (1972), p.3.
6. quoted in May (1978), p.120.
7. Claude Blake 'Chinese Vice in England' *The Sunday Chronicle*, Dec. 2nd, 1906, quoted in Waller (1970).
8. quoted in May (1978), p.118.
9. quoted in Waller (1970).
10. quoted in May (1978), p.119
11. ibid., p.119.
12. ibid., p.119.

Chapter 2
Of Opium and Coolies: Sino-British Relations in the 19th Century

1. A. Lindley *The Taiping Heavenly Kingdom* (1866) quoted in Clark and Gregory (1982), p.417.
2. quoted in Hookham (1972), p. 274.
3. quoted in Hayter (1981), pp19-20.
4. quoted in Guan Shijie (1987), p.19.
5. quoted in Hibbert (1984), p. 241.
6. quoted in Hibbert (1984), p.266.
7. According to Pan (1990), p45, the word 'coolie' originally derived from an aboriginal tribe in India, and was extended to mean transient labour or hireling. It contributed to a new Chinese word — kuli — meaning 'bitter strength'.
8. quoted in Thaxton (1983), p.32.
9. quoted in Campbell (1923), p.4.
10. from W. Reeves' preface to Campbell (1923), p.xiii.
11. quoted in Berridge (1978), p.15.

12. quoted in ibid., p.8.
13. from *The Times*, Nov. 22nd, 1878, in May (1978), p.113.
14. from *The Times*, Aug. 25th, 1877 in ibid., p.112.

Chapter 3
Race Riots and Revolution: relations between the British and Chinese in the early 20th Century

1. from *The Times*, April 9th, 1966 quoted in Summerskill (1982), p.206.
2. quoted in May (1978), p116.
3. from the *North China Daily Herald*, June 8th, 1918, quoted in Summerskill (1982), p.132.
4. from Allen Hutt *The Post-War History of the British Working Class* (Victor Gollancz, 1937) quoted in Fryer (1985), p.312.
5. Fryer (1985), p.312.

Chapter 4
The Chinese in Britain today: media images and real lives

1. A. Chan *A Report on the Employment Prospects of Chinese Youth in Britain* CRE, July 1986.
2. Pan (1990), p. 355.
3. reviewed in *SiYu* No. 27, April 1990.
4. 'Violence at Thurrock Restaurants' Essex Community Relations Council reviewed in *SiYu* No. 26, Dec. 1989.
5. Jabez Lam 'Racism Brings Collective Action' in *China Now* No. 199, Summer, 1989.
6. The case of the Diamond Four is discussed in *SiYu* No. 19, Nov.1987.
7. Norman Tebbit is quoted in *The Sun*, Dec. 22nd, 1989.
8. The MPs are quoted by Emily Lau reporting in the *Far Eastern Economic Review*, Dec. 28th, 1989, p.11.

Bibliography

Banton, M. and Harwood, J. (1975) *The Race Concept.* David & Charles

Berridge, V. (1978) 'East End Opium Dens and Narcotic Use in Britain' *The London Journal,* Vol. 4., No. 1, pp.3-28

Booth, M. (1990) *The Triads: the Chinese Criminal Fraternity.* Grafton Books

Campbell, P. C. (1923) *Chinese Coolie Emigration.* P. S. King & Son

Chan, A. (1986) *A Report on the Employment Prospects of Chinese Youth in Britain.* CRE, July 1986

Chesneaux, J. (1973) *Peasant Revolts in China 1840-1949,* Thames and Hudson

Clark, P. and Gregory, J. S. (1982) *Western Reports on the Taiping.* Croom Helm

Essex Community Relations Council (1989) *Violence in Thurrock Restaurants.*

Fryer, P (1985) *Staying Power: The History of Black People in Britain.* Pluto Press

Glover, D. 'The Sociology of Mass Media' in M. Haralambos (ed.) *Sociology: New Directions.* Causeway Books, pp. 371-445

Guan Shijie (1987) 'Chartism and the First Opium War' *History Workshop Journal,* Issue 24, Autumn, pp. 17-31

Hall, S., *et al* (1978) *Policing the Crisis.* MacMillan

Hayter, T. (1981) *The Creation of World Poverty.* Pluto Press

Hibbert, C. (1984) *The Dragon Wakes: China and the West, 1793- 1911.* Penguin

Hookham, H. (1972) *A Short History of China.* Mentor Books

Huang, P. (1985) *The Peasant Economy and Social Change in North China.* Stanford University Press

Lam, J. (1989) 'Racism brings collective action', *China Now* No. 129, Summer

Marx, K. and Engels, F. (1976) *On Colonialism.* Lawrence and Wishart

May, J. P. (1978) 'The Chinese in Britain: 1860-1914' in C. Holmes (ed)., *Immigrants and Minorities in British Society.* Allen and Unwin

Pan, L. (1990) *Sons of the Yellow Emperor: the Story of the Overseas Chinese.* Secker and Warburg

Shang, A. (1984) *The Chinese in Britain,* Batsford Educational

Sivanandan, A. (1985) 'RAT and the degradation of black struggle' *Race & Class* Vol. XXVI, No. 4, Spring

Summerskill, M. (1982) *China on the Western Front*. M. Summerskill

Tam, H. (1985) 'Home Affairs and Britain's Chinese', *China Now* No. 113, Summer

Thaxton, R. *China Turned Rightside Up*. Yale University Press

Van Ash, C. and Sax Rohmer, E. (1972) *Master of Villainy: a biography of Sax Rohmer*. Tom Stacey

Waller, P. J. (1970) 'Racial Phobia: The Chinese Scare 1906-1914' in *Essays Presented to C.M.Bowra*. The Alden Press for Wadham College

Waller, P. J. (1985) 'Immigration into Britain: The Chinese', *History Today*, Vol. 35, Sept

Wu, W. (1982) *The Yellow Peril: Chinese Americans in American Film Fiction, 1850-1940*. Archon Books